D0497784

DRAWING ARCHAEOLOGICAL FINDS

DRAWING ARCHAEOLOGICAL FINDS

by
CONANT BRODRIBB

Association Press
New York

DRAWING ARCHAEOLOGICAL FINDS

First American Edition 1971
Copyright © Text and Illustrations 1970 Conant Brodribb

Association Press, 291 Broadway, New York, N. Y. 10007

All rights reserved. No part of this publication may be reprinted, reproduced, transmitted, stored in a retrieval system, or otherwise utilized, in any form or by any means, electronic or mechanical, including photocopying or recording, now existing or hereinafter invented, without the prior written permission of the publisher.

Standard Book Number: 8096-1806-0
Library of Congress Catalog Card Number: 74-129434

Printed in the United States of America

CONTENTS

PREFACE

The purpose of this book is to help student and amateur archaeologists to acquire a basic archaeological skill, preparing drawings of finds for reproduction. The beginner may feel he cannot draw even a reasonably straight line but one day he may have to draw finds for reproduction because no one else will do it for him. Exchanging trowel for pen can be a laborious and daunting task if one does not know the rudiments, but a pleasurable challenge if one does.

It is impossible and futile to try to lay down detailed rules for drawing finds. The choice of a suitable technique may depend entirely on the characteristics of the object to be drawn and there can be many different satisfactory solutions to the problem of representing a particular find. Drawing is an individual and personal activity and in this specialized form of still-life illustration one method can be just as successful as another. There are, however, certain fundamental precepts for ensuring successful reproduction of drawings and I have tried to show how these may be applied. The results may, I hope, be of some service to beginners in search of guidance. Some points may seem very elementary; they are nonetheless important.

7

Although most of the drawings are of objects of the Roman-British period, I hope that prehistorians, medievalists and industrial archaeologists will find something useful in them. The problems of drawing, for effective reproduction, a flint scraper, a bronze dagger, an enameled brooch, a bone comb and a windmill are, when it comes to putting pen to paper, very much the same.

I am indebted to my friends Dr. Anthony Hands and Mr. David Walker for their permission to use illustrations which we have together published elsewhere, and for their helpful suggestions. I am also grateful to many others for their interest and kindness, in particular Mr. Edward Rimes and Mr. Christopher Foss for help with printing technicalities, and Mrs. Barbara Bunyan for typing the manuscript. I am especially grateful for my wife for her constant encouragement.

Conant Brodribb

DRAWING ARCHAEOLOGICAL FINDS

INTRODUCTION

All archaeologists know their duty to publish their finds. In these days of high printing costs they are also under the obligation to make the best use possible of whatever space may be available for publication. Today, a few pages in a local archaeological society's journal may well be all the detailed publication an important site and its finds will ever receive. Finds may go to a distant museum: they may be lost, destroyed or stolen, but if good illustrations of them have been published their inaccessibility or loss may not matter very much because the illustrations can be consulted. An illustration can often explain a find better than a long description, and if we accept the old Chinese proverb that "one picture is worth more than ten thousand words of description," we should try to ensure that the picture is good. A bad picture is a disservice to the reader. He may be undertaking research into a certain class of find and needing to familiarize himself fully with its detailed features; he may be an excavator searching for a published example of an object he has found. A bad picture will not help him.

11

What is a "good" picture of an archaeological find? It should be a clear, accurate, neat, objective and impersonal record. Figure 1A, a not uncommon type of archaeological illustration, gives us a certain amount of information about the nature of the find, but rather crudely. If we can draw Figure 1A we can also draw Figure 1B—which says a good deal more about the shape, structure and texture of the find—without any more expense, without much more effort and certainly without years of training. No great artistic skill is needed, only a knowledge of simple tools and methods and basic printing processes. The archaeological draftsman is not drawing to express his soul or for exhibition but to impart information which will be reproduced by printing. This means using methods and techniques not normally used in drawing for pleasure. His drawings are reproduced, usually at a size different from that at which they were drawn, by mechanical processes over which he has no control, and in order to get good results he needs to know how these processes work. They cannot get more (and, if care is not taken, may well get much less) out of a drawing than has been put into it.

Illustrations in archaeological reports are printed by several different methods, the cheapest and most common being line engravings made from pen and ink drawings, as in these pages. Lithography and halftone engravings are also used, the latter for the reproduction of photographs.

• Line Engravings

A line engraving can be described as a copy of a black and white drawing made on metal so that it can be printed

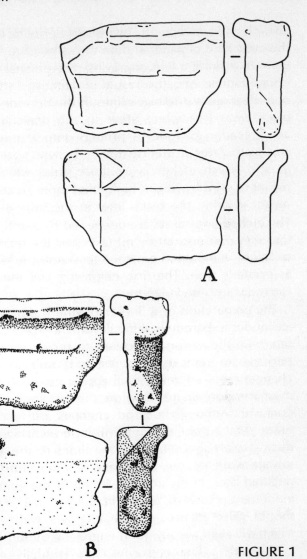

A

B

FIGURE 1

cheaply and conveniently by the same printing process, on the same kind of paper and on the same page as printer's type. In making a line engraving, the original drawing is photographed and the resulting negative, which shows only clear areas (the black lines in the drawing) and solid black areas (the white areas in the drawing), without any gradation of tone, is printed onto a prepared thin zinc plate. After further treatment the zinc plate is washed in acid which etches away those areas which are not meant to print leaving in high relief those areas which are meant to print (the black lines in the original drawing). The etched-away areas are deepened by a drill, to ensure that they do not print by mistake, and the finished plate, or "zinc," is mounted on wood to exactly the same height as printer's type. The line engraving and the text type can then be printed together.

The preparation of a line engraving is purely mechanical and it is extremely difficult for the engraver to interfere with the various processes to rectify errors except, perhaps, to remove an unwanted, isolated line. Any changes required in the final appearance of the drawing must therefore be made before the drawing is sent to the engraver. Although a good engraver can do much to ensure that a poor drawing will have a chance of reproducing tolerably well, there are limits to the amount of salvage work he can undertake and his efforts may be nullified later, in the actual printing of the engraving, by indifferent presswork or unsuitable paper. The draftsman should strive to provide the engraver with a drawing which will yield a really good engraving without difficulty.

Although a line engraving will faithfully reproduce

black lines, dots and masses, it cannot reproduce grays or shades between pure black and pure white. For example, pencil shading added to an ink drawing will, if heavy, be reproduced by a line engraving as solid black; if very light, it will be "seen" by the engraver's camera as white and will not reproduce at all. A drawing for a

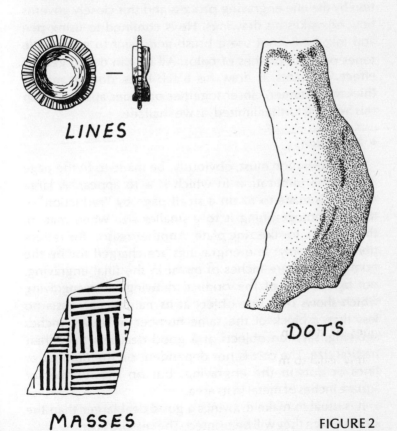

LINES

DOTS

MASSES   FIGURE 2 line engraving cannot, therefore, contain any actual gradations of tone, but illusions of tone can be given by careful juxtaposition of the only two tones at the draftsman's command—the black of the printing ink and the white of the page on which the engraving is printed. The draftsman can use only lines, dots or masses (Figure 2) for reproduction by the line engraving process and this closely governs how he makes his drawings. He is confined to using pen· and ink; he cannot use a brush and paint to give subtle tones or vivid splashes of color. All he can do, to get the effects he wants, is draw his black lines, dots or masses thicker or thinner, closer together or wider apart—and in this he is still further limited, as we shall see.

• Reduction

Any illustration must, obviously, be made to fit the page size of the publication in which it is to appear. A large drawing is made to fit on a small page by "reduction"—that is, photographing it to a smaller size when making the negative for the zinc plate. Another reason for reduction is economy: line engravings are charged for by the number of square inches of metal in the final engraving, not by the size of the original drawing. An engraving which shows only one object at its natural size costs no less than a block of the same number of square inches showing, say, ten objects at a good deal less than their natural size. The cost is not dependent on the number of lines or dots in the engraving, but on the number of square inches of metal in its area.

It is usual to make drawings a good deal larger than the size at which they will be printed. The reasons are:

1. To allow for reduction to fit several possible page sizes.

2. Because it is much easier to draw detail accurately at a large size than to try to do so on a very small scale (Figure 3).

3. To improve the appearance of the drawing.

Reduction in size improves a drawing by "sharpening it up," making thick lines thin, and clumsy lines seem neater. This "sharpening," however, sets a trap for the un-

Actual size ($^1/_1$): no pen can draw lines as thin and close as these.

As drawn at $^2/_1$

FIGURE 3

LINE THICKNESS

Line
1/200 of
an inch —
0.125 mm. —
thick. This is
the thinnest line
which the line engraving
process will safely
reproduce.

Line
1/50 of an
inch — 0.5 mm. —
thick. This is
the thinnest line
which will reproduce
safely when reduced
to 1/4 linear.

FIGURE 4

wary. When a drawing is reduced in size, all the lines in it are inevitably reduced as well. Thus a line drawn 1/100 of an inch thick is reduced to a thickness of 1/200 of an inch when the drawing undergoes linear reduction to a half. The technical term "linear reduction" should always be used when specifying or considering a degree of reduction, to distinguished it from "area reduction" which is quite different. A drawing 4 in. X 2 in. comes out at 2 in. X 1 in. when reduced to 1/2 linear, although its actual area is reduced not to 1/2 but to 1/4, from 8 sq. in. to only 2 sq. in. The term "reduction" used in these pages refers only to "linear" reduction.

Most of the drawings in this book are printed unreduced to enable details of construction to be shown clearly. Those that have been reduced show the effect of "sharpening up."

The thinnest line which can be effectively reproduced in the metal of a line engraving without either flawing in manufacture or breaking in printing is 1/200 of an inch, 0.125 mm. (Figure 4). This naturally affects the thickness of the lines put into the original drawing. If a drawing is to be reproduced at a linear reduction to a quarter of its original size and the thinnest permissible line in the block is 1/200 of an inch, the thinnest permissible line in the original drawing must be four times as thick as 1/200 of an inch—that is, 1/50 of an inch, or 0.5 mm.

Lines drawn very close together in an original may, when the drawing is reduced for reproduction, "fill in" or merge, printing not as thin separate lines but as a thick black blob. The original drawing must therefore be kept "open," with lines spaced sufficiently far apart to prevent

EFFECTS OF REDUCTION

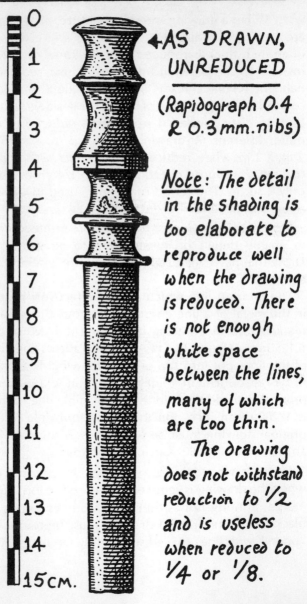

← AS DRAWN, UNREDUCED

(Rapidograph 0.4 & 0.3 mm. nibs)

Note: The detail in the shading is too elaborate to reproduce well when the drawing is reduced. There is not enough white space between the lines, many of which are too thin.

The drawing does not withstand reduction to ½ and is useless when reduced to ¼ or ⅛.

← REDUCED TO ½

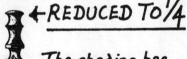

Detail in the
shading has
filled in and
the isolated
dots have
become very
faint.

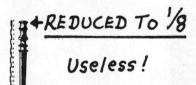

← REDUCED TO ¼

The shading has
turned to solid
black; the isolated
dots have vanished.

← REDUCED TO ⅛

Useless!

FIGURE 5

ALLOWING FOR REDUCTION

←AS DRAWN,
UNREDUCED

(Rapidograph 0.5mm. nib)

Note: All lines are of uniform thickness, drawn boldly with a thick nib, and spaced fairly widely apart. There is no fine detail and no attempt at any elaborate treatment.

In spite of this, however, the drawing appears at its best when reduced to only ½. This kind of drawing cannot be made to reduce equally well to both ½ and ¼ of its original size.

← REDUCED TO ½

All the lines in
the drawing are
clear and remain
individually
distinguishable
at this size.

← REDUCED TO ¼

Some shading turns
to solid black but
some of it remains
fairly open.

← REDUCED TO ⅛

Useless!

FIGURE 6

them from filling in on reduction. Finely drawn detail can
be marred or lost altogether if the degree of reduction is
great and proper allowance has not been made for this
(Figures 5 and 6).

● Sizing of Drawings

It is important for the draftsman to know the size at
which his drawing is to be published and the degree of
reduction for which he must allow. He may be unable to
start work at all if he cannot obtain this essential information from the director of the excavation or from the
editor of the journal in which the drawing is to appear,
and he must press for a definite decision. There are, however, certain accepted conventions of scale at which finds
are published. Most small objects are published at natural
size. If they contain much detail, it is best to draw them
at 2/1 so that reduction by a half brings them down to
1/1. It is much easier to work out exact measurements for
drawing an object at twice its actual size than for drawing it at one and a half times its size. Drawings are custo-
marily reduced in plate-making to 1/2 or 1/4 or occasionally 1/3, or 2/3 or 1/5 or 3/5 but very seldom to odd fractions such as 3/8 or 2/5. A good general rule is to draw
small finds at 2/1 for reduction to 1/1 unless the publication in which the drawing is to appear has an editorial
rule that drawings will be reduced to, say, 1/3, in which
case drawings can be made at 1/1 if this is convenient.
Certain classes of find—e.g. Roman ironwork—are often
published at 1/4, in which case they can be drawn at 1/1
or even 1/2. Large finds, e.g. stonework such as roof slates,
millstones or column capitals, are often published at

1/8, in which case they can be drawn at 1/1 or, to avoid an inconveniently large drawing, at 1/2 or even 1/4. It is, of course, much quicker, if less accurate, to draw an object at 1/2 than, say, 1/1, if it is to be published at 1/4: a much smaller area of paper has to be covered by the pen. A very small object may need to be published at twice its actual size if all detail is to be clearly shown: in such a case it may be best to draw it at 4/1 for reduction to 2/1.

● Offset Lithography

Offset lithography, another printing method of reproducing line drawings, needs to be mentioned. It is enough to say that, although it involves a process completely different from that of the line engraving (viz, printing from a flat metal or plastic sheet) the preparation of a drawing for reproduction by offset lithography should be regarded as subject to exactly the same considerations of line thickness, reduction and "open" drawing as for the line engraving process.

TOOLS AND MATERIALS

Apart from a table at which to work and an adjustable lamp (to be discussed later), the essential tools and materials for producing pen and ink drawings of archaeological finds are a pencil, an eraser, a ruler, a set square, ink, a pen, paper, and a means of correcting errors in pen work. Not absolutely essential, but extremely useful, are a drawing compass, dividers, a small water-color paintbrush (for inking in large areas of solid black), a magnifying glass, and a means of checking the effect of reduction on drawings.

● **Pencils**

Any good HB pencil will serve. Very cheap pencils are difficult to sharpen well and often have gritty, scratchy leads. The harder grades of pencil, H to 6H, give very thin lines, which may, however, score the paper, making subsequent ink work difficult. Ink will take well only on an undamaged, clean, paper surface. The softer grades, B to 6B, give lines which are too thick for subsequent pen work and tend to smear when erased. A metal "clutch" pencil, with a built-in sharpener, may be found better than a wooden pencil. It is heavier, which is an aid to steadiness in drawing, and it is easily sharpened. A sharp pencil makes for precision, and precision in the initial pencil work in a drawing is most important, particularly for a beginner.

● **Erasers**

A fairly soft white India rubber or plastic eraser is best; the cheapest kinds may spoil the paper surface for ink work. An eraser should be cut in half diagonally, giving it chisel edges and points for making small accurate corrections. It should be kept clean and used gently; on some papers vigorous erasing may ruin the surface for ink work.

● **Ink**

India ink should always be used. It is dense, of even consistency (which is important for consistent line work), and water proof. If a special drawing pen is being used, the India ink recommended by the makers should be used with it.

● **Paper**

Smooth white nonabsorbent paper is best. Textured, grainy paper may seem attractive, but breaks up pen strokes, which can lead to difficulties in making an engraving. Good quality smooth white writing paper is excellent; so, if the best grades are used, is white tracing paper. Tracing paper, however, buckles if large areas of solid black are inked on it. Some cheap papers cannot withstand much use of the eraser or become pulpy if their surfaces are scratched up by the pen nib. The best results of all are given by Bristol board, a laminated, extremely smooth white sheet. It is not cheap, but is well worth using if only a few drawings, or drawings involving much fine detail, are required.

For certain tasks, faint blue lined graph paper can be used (see p. 62).

Instead of paper or board, plastic sheets such as prepared acetate, mylar or Cronaflex can be used, but these are expensive and may require the use of special acetate inks. Whatever paper is to be used should be stored in a warm, dry, clean place. If it is stored in a damp room or even in a cold room in winter, it will absorb moisture and drawings made on it will look as if they have been made on blotting paper. Paper should be brushed before use to ensure an absolutely clean working surface.

● Pens

We can use "dip" pens with nibs which fit into separate penholders and need to be dipped into an ink bottle, ordinary fountain pens, or special precision drawing pens. Ball-point and felt- or fibre-tipped pens are not suitable; the former smear, the latter give too coarse a line and both use the wrong kind of ink.

● "Dip" Pens

The ordinary "dip" pen, which may have a small ink reservoir in either the holder or the nib, is cheap and needs skill in use. Its flow of ink is seldom controllable and it tends to run dry at the most inconvenient moment, usually in mid-line. Broken pen strokes reproduce badly in a line engraving. An open ink bottle is dangerously easy to knock over, too. If we use a "dip" pen, we need a strong, fairly large firm nib. The tiny "crow quill" or mapping pen nib is difficult and tedious to use for freehand or large-scale drawing. It tends to catch in the paper and splatter little ink blots all over the drawing.

The main disadvantage of the "dip" nib is that it is very difficult to gauge the right thickness of line to withstand a particular degree of reduction. A nib which varies its thickness of line according to the pressure put on it is not the best choice for a beginner.

● Fountain Pens

The ordinary fountain pen also presents its user with the difficulty of hitting on the right pressure for the right thickness of line. It is excellent for use with inks which are not waterproof, but soon clogs if India ink is used in it. Like the "dip" pen, it is best avoided by a beginner.

● Precision Drawing Pens

For consistently even results (which are important for making good engravings or if a number of separate drawings are to be incorporated into one text figure or shown on the same page), the best pens are precision drawing pens, of which several different kinds are available. The most useful of these are the Rotring Rapidograph or Rapidograph Variant, the Pelikan Technos and the Pelikan Graphos. Each offers peculiar advantages, but in general the Rapidograph Variant or the Pelikan Technos (both are stylus pens) seem to be best for the beginner and the Graphos more suited to the more experienced hand. Each pen consists of a holder, a capacious ink reservoir with controlled feed, and a range of nibs. Specialist accessories, such as stenciling nibs and compass attachments, are also available. Because new or improved models of these instruments come on the market at fairly frequent intervals, it is advisable to consult the makers' latest catalogues for details as to the range of pens, nibs and accessories.

The Rapidograph Variant

A Rapidograph Variant nib (or "cone") is a hardened steel tube, containing a thin steel rod, which gives a firm, wiry line of unvarying thickness. The range of nibs offers 10 different thicknesses of line, from 0.1 mm. to 1.2 mm. Differences in line thickness cannot be obtained by varying the pressure of the hand or by altering the angle of the pen but only by switching to another nib. Thus a nib designed to give a line 0.4 mm. thick cannot be induced to give a line 0.6 mm. thick except by making two pen strokes merge or overlap. If a really accurate line 0.6 mm. thick is required, a 0.6 mm. nib must be used. This means that a drawing requiring precise thick, medium and thin lines requires the use of several different nibs. Subtle variations of thickness within any one line cannot be achieved with any one nib but, because the nib is tubular, the pen does not need to be rotated in the hand to maintain an even thickness of line when drawing a curve or a circle.

Although the Rapidograph is not a very sensitive pen, it is capable of extremely good work. It produces a bold, clear line which is encouraging and gives confidence. Its

performance is consistent and after a while the user will
know exactly what he can expect from it, which will
then leave him free to concentrate on drawing without
fearing sudden tantrums on the part of the pen. For a
beginner—or a left-handed draftsman—it is excellent.

RAPIDOGRAPH PEN

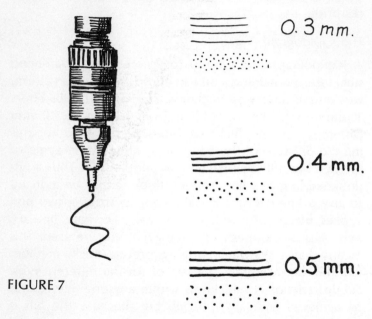

0. 3 mm.

0.4 mm.

0.5 mm.

FIGURE 7

The tubular nib is, however, incapable of starting or end-
ing a line with a square point; all its lines have round ends
and this can be noticeable when using the thickest nibs.

The Rapidograph nib holder has a diameter similar to
that of an ordinary fountain pen, and the weight is toward

the point—a feature which makes it easy to hold and control the pen. A separate nib unit, with its own reservoir, nib and protective cap, can be screwed into each end and left permanently in place.

If drawings are to be reduced to only 1/2 linear, three different nibs should suffice: 0.3 mm. for the finest detail, 0.4 mm. for general work, and 0.5 mm. or 0.6 mm. for the thickest lines. One can, however, play safe by using a 0.4 mm. nib for the finest detail, a 0.6 mm. for general work and an 0.8 mm. for the thickest lines (Figure 7). If greater variation in degrees of reduction is likely, with some drawings to be reduced to as little as 1/8 of original size, more than three different nibs may be needed.

Because the thinnest permissible line in a normal line engraving is 1/200 of an inch, the thinnest nibs which can be safely used for any degree of reduction are: for linear reduction to 1/8, 1.0 mm.; to 1/6, 0.8 mm.; to 1/4, 0.5 mm.; to 1/3, 0.4 mm.; to 1/2, 0.3 mm. Again, one can play safe by using the next larger size of nib suggested for each degree of reduction shown above (0.4 mm. instead of 0.3 mm. for reduction to 1/2, and so on).

The Pelikan Technos

Although its construction is different, the Technos pen is of the same basic kind as the Rapidograph, employing a wide range of inflexible steel tube or blade nibs (or "points") of different line thicknesses for drawing, lettering and ruling. The best for freehand drawing are the C range, 0.3, 0.4, 0.5 and 0.6 mm. in line thickness (Figure 8). The nib units are more convenient to change than those of the Rapidograph and the ink feed regulator,

TECHNOS PEN

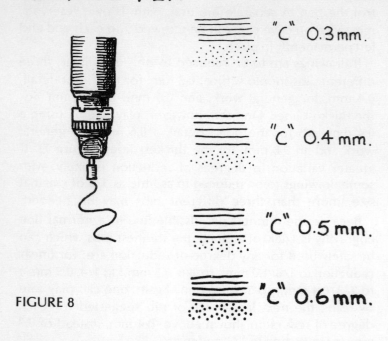

"C" 0.3 mm.

"C" 0.4 mm.

"C" 0.5 mm.

FIGURE 8

'C" 0.6 mm.

which is designed for use with ink cartridges only, is an integral part of the penholder. Because of their general similarity, all of what has been said above about the use of the Rapidograph—line thickness or reduction and so forth—applies also to the use of the Technos. There is hardly anything to choose between them for general drawing purposes. A Technos nib is not as hard-wearing or as smooth in use as a Rapidograph nib, but it is cheaper, and is free of the Rapidograph nib's occasional vice of making a tiny blob at the beginning or end of a line.

The Pelikan Graphos

The Pelikan Graphos pen offers to the fairly experienced draftsman a number of advantages over the Rapidograph or Technos, particularly for freehand drawing. Its series of nibs (some 60 in all) is most comprehensive, ranging from those which produce work of mapping pen fineness to those designed for bold lettering. Within certain limits, one nib will yield variations in line thickness according to the pressure employed because it is flexible and not a rigid tube.

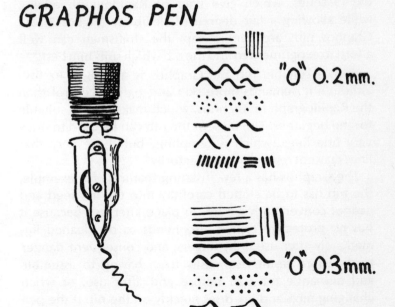

GRAPHOS PEN

"0" 0.2mm.

"0" 0.3mm.

FIGURE 9

Graphos nibs are very cheap, but the holder, which contains the built-in reservoir and ink feed, is expensive. The ink feed is made in three different types according to the rate of flow desired, but for all general work the no. 2 feed is the most suitable. The nibs recommended by the makers for fine freehand drawing are extremely flexible and rather difficult for the beginner to control. They are meant for artistic rather than technical drawing and give lines which may be too fine for good reproduction by a line engraving. Two of the most suitable nibs for drawing archaeological finds are the 0.2 mm. and the 0.3 mm. in the O series, which give lines of Rapidograph quality while allowing a fair degree of flexibility (Figure 9). As Graphos nibs are very cheap, the draftsman can well afford to experiment to find the nib which suits him best.

With a suitable nib the Graphos is a delight to use, although it demands more skill and tighter control than the Rapidograph or Technos, which makes it less suitable for the beginner. The back of the nib can be used to draw very fine lines, which is tempting, but these very thin lines may not reproduce satisfactorily.

The Graphos has a few irritating features: for example, the nib has to be slotted carefully into the ink feed and cannot conveniently be left in place after use because it has no protective cap. It also needs to be cleaned immediately after use. Inky fingers, and consequent danger to drawings, result very easily from having to assemble and dismantle the pen before and after use, or when changing nibs, and ink dries quickly on the nib if the pen is left idle for more than a few minutes during use. The holder is slimmer than that of the Rapidograph or Technos,

PENS AND NIBS COMPARED

Drawings and captions on cartridge
at 2/1, reduced here to 1/1.

RAPIDOGRAPH 0.5MM.   TECHNOS "C" 0.5MM.

RAPIDOGRAPH 0.4MM.   TECHNOS "C" 0.4 MM.

GRAPHOS "O" 0.3MM. (Medium pressure)

GRAPHOS "O" 0.3MM. (Light pressure)

GRAPHOS "O" 0.2MM. (Medium pressure)

GRAPHOS "O" 0.2MM. (light pressure)

FIGURE 10

which may be tiring to the fingers or a cause of poor
control of the pen, but this can be overcome by wrapping
adhesive tape round it to thicken it to a more convenient
diameter.

• Which Pen to Choose?

For most practical purposes there is little to choose between the Rapidograph, the Technos and the Graphos, as
will be apparent from Figure 10. The Rapidograph, however, seems specially suited to the beginner because it
handles easily.

• Measuring Equipment

Drawings must be accurately set out if they are to be
accurate representations of finds. Not much equipment is
needed. A large transparent set square with beveled
edges is essential, as is a clear plastic ruler marked in
inches and millimeters. Millimeters are much more convenient to use than fractions of an inch when transfering
measurements of an object to paper. A compass for
drawing circles in pencil is most useful: it may not be
required often but it is difficult to improvise a substitute
at short notice. Dividers are useful for very accurate
measurement and should have a good spread when
fully extended.

• Correcting Errors

To the beginner, an error in pen and ink work may seem
an irreparable disaster, but it can be put right very easily
by pasting it over with a fresh piece of paper or by painting it out and drawing again on the new surface. It is a

comforting thought that corrections of this kind, which would look bad on a drawing intended for exhibition, are a matter of complete indifference to the engraver's camera. The camera can "see" only the black lines of the drawing, and not where white paper or white paint has has been superimposed. An error does not therefore matter; one wobbly line does not mean having to start the whole drawing again.

PAINTING OUT

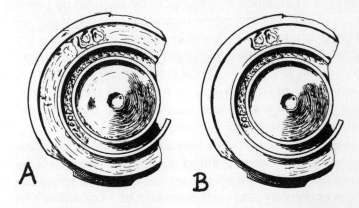

A

B

The original drawing, unmodified.

After modification with process white.

FIGURE 11

Pasting-over is convenient for rectifying large-scale errors; for small errors or general "cleaning up," either process white, a water-based paint applied like water-color, or a petroleum-based paint such as Snopake, is handy (Figure 11). Process white is cheap but can take a long time to dry if applied thickly and no redrawing can be done on it until it is really dry. Snopake is much more expensive but dries hard in a matter of seconds (breathing on it helps to dry it faster). A pen line drawn over process white or Snopake may, however, turn out rather thicker than intended (Figure 12). This may necessitate a further correction which, if it is still faulty, can be painted out again and redrawn. If the surface of the paper has been damaged by vigorous erasing, it can be restored by painting over with process white or Snopake, but ink put on either process white or Snopake takes a long time to dry thoroughly and a corrected drawing should be put aside carefully to prevent its being accidentally smudged. A drawing can go to the engraver looking like a patchwork quilt of pastings-over and paintings-out but will still make a good engraving.

The brush supplied with Snopake is too thick for accurate work and a thin, pointed water-color brush will be found better. One defect of Snopake is that the screw cap of the bottle may clog with paint and be very difficult to undo. Accumulations of dried Snopake in the threads of the cap should be scraped off and put back in the bottle where they will dissolve and become usable again.

For pasting on new patches of paper a rubber cement is best. A patch may need to be peeled off again; it may be very difficult to remove without damaging the drawing

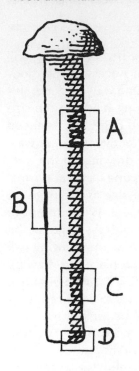

In the squares A-D the original drawing was painted out with Snopake, very thickly applied, on which new lines were drawn before it was fully dry. Note how the new lines have thickened, even though the same nib was used.

FIGURE 12

if impact adhesives are used. The edges of a patch should be painted over with process white or Snopake: a thick patch can cast a slight shadow in plate-making which may reproduce as a black line, and erasing surplus rubber cement may also leave a black line.

On laminated Bristol board corrections can be made by cutting out the error with a razor blade and drawing on the new surface revealed below. On plastic sheet an error can be scraped out with a knife, but knife-work on paper ruins the surface for further drawing.

● Optical Equipment

It is very helpful to be able to judge how a drawing will look after reduction so that it can, if necessary, be modified before it goes to the engraver. One way of doing this is to have a photograph of the drawing made to the size at which it will appear on the printed page, e.g. reduced to 1/4 linear. This is expensive but effective. Another way, rather rough and ready, is to pin the drawing on the wall, and back away from it, holding up in one hand, at normal reading distance, a page of the same size as the page on which the drawing will ultimately appear. When the page in the hand is seen to coincide in size with the page on the wall, a rough idea will be gained of how the drawing will look when reduced. Similarly, one can place the drawing on the floor, and stand on a chair to view it from a distance.

The most convenient way, however, is to use a reducing glass through which the drawing will be seen at half size. Reducing glasses are not expensive and can be obtained from opticians and scientific instrument shops.

A magnifying glass obviously is useful for examining detail in objects to be drawn. Occasionally useful are dark glasses, or a photographic dark blue "pan vision" filter, through which a brightly colored object can be seen in subdued tones, thus allowing the draftsman to concentrate on analyzing and reproducing the pattern of light and shade in the object without being distracted by the colors. This is useful when drawing, for example, a bronze object with a bright green patina and complex detail.

TECHNIQUES OF DRAWING FINDS

Now that we know what we are trying to do, how our drawings will be reproduced, and what tools and materials to use, we can begin to make a drawing. All excavation, it has been said, is destruction; all illustration, it might be said, is approximation. A line drawing of a find is a two-dimensional representation of a three-dimensional object, and can be only an approximation to reality. A line, after all, is really an abstraction, a convention for representing an invisible boundary between two surfaces. Every draftsman has, or will develop, his own methods of approaching the reality he is trying to represent, but certain general rules can be observed to advantage.

A realistic, almost photographically explicit style of drawing is required (Figure 13). An impressionist style is unsuitable because detail is important and must be fully expressed, not merely hinted at. The need for simplicity should not, however, be forgotten in the quest for realism —simplicity leads to good reproduction of a drawing. Economy of line is desirable if it can be achieved: every

Realism versus impressionism. A may be dull but is a better <u>archaeological</u> drawing than B.

FIGURE 13

line should have a definite meaning and purpose. If a line adds nothing it should be eliminated. "If in doubt, leave out" is a sound maxim when drawing for reproduction, provided that no significant feature is thereby omitted.

● Careful Observation

The first part of making a drawing is careful observation. What is the nature, purpose and composition of the thing to be drawn? The draftsman faced with an incomprehensible object should ask the director of the excavation or some other competent person what it is and what features of it, if any, should be emphasized, specially shown or ignored. A lump of corrosion on an iron object may or may not be important; it may be a freak of oxidization or the remains of a significant feature such as a stud or a hinge. Where identification is impossible the object should be drawn exactly as it appears to the eye, "warts and all." If, after laboratory treatment new features are revealed, the drawing can be altered; if the object crumbles before conservation, the first drawing will at least be a fair record of it.

Observation should not be hurried. Figure 14 shows what can happen if it is. A is a reasonable drawing of a small bronze object, but does not tell the whole story. The draftsman failed to examine the find really closely; he was in a hurry and did not notice the patterns under the surface corrosion. B, not A, is the true representation of the find. The time spent drawing A was therefore largely wasted except that the basic outline of A proved suitable for the basic outline of B, which saved a certain

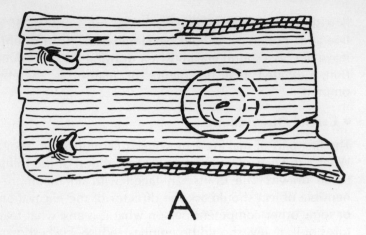

A

B

FIGURE 14

amount of redrawing. Note the change of style to show the extra detail. In a sense B is not as exact representation because the patterns were very faint; but they were extremely important features and therefore had to be made quite clear in the drawing, even if this meant some emphasis when compared with the original.

A badly damaged or fragmentary find can, if its identification is absolutely certain, be shown as complete by outlining the missing parts in dotted lines. This should not be done if there is any doubt about the nature of the missing parts, and is largely a matter for discretion. There can be no general rule about it.

The find to be drawn should be studied carefully under a strong side light as this will often reveal features which are invisible under frontal lighting. It is customary to draw all finds as if lit from above and to the left. This convention shows their structure, modeling and texture to best advantage. It is also a convenience to the draftsman in that he can make his drawings at whatever hour he pleases, by artificial light, without needing good daylight. A lamp of the Luxo or Dazor kind is most useful because it can be adjusted to give the best lighting for the effect required and can be left in place with the object set up below it if drawing is interrupted for any reason. A firm, solid table on which to draw is essential. A drawing board is a convenience, but a pad of paper will serve just as well.

• Style of Drawing

The next steps are consideration of the style of drawing to be employed and accurate measurement of the object.

A rough sketch and written notes at this point may save much time later on. If several separate drawings are to be grouped together in one text figure, they should be consistent in style. In general, a beginner will find it best to make a completely detailed pencil drawing before beginning any ink work. By so doing, he can make any necessary corrections or adjustments easily and conveniently with an eraser as the construction of the drawing proceeds. Although the pencil work may take a long time to complete, the subsequent ink work will not take long. Putting ink on a detailed pencil "skeleton" enables the beginner to concentrate on making suitable unbroken pen strokes without having to keep taking his eyes off his drawing to look at his subject. Once experience has been gained with the pen, much preliminary pencil work can be omitted. When making a detailed preliminary pencil drawing, only lines should be used, with no shaded tones to indicate modeling. It is a waste of time and effort to put delicate gradations of shading in the pencil drawing because the effect achieved cannot be reproduced in ink or by the line engraving. In the very last stages of a pencil drawing,

Correct

Incorrect

FIGURE 15

the position and strength of shadows should be noted lightly as a guide to subsequent ink shading. The pencil should be used so that it draws lightly, not heavily. It should not be held too near the point, with the thumb and fingers sharply bent, because this is tiring and also obscures the line being drawn (Figure 15).

If at first great difficulty is found in drawing a neat straight line, a ruler should be used. It is better to be accurate, even if mechanical, than vague. With experience, the ruler will become unnecessary. In the same way, if drawing a steady curved line is difficult, a compass can be used. There is, of course, no room for imprecision. Every pencil line must be capable of accurate translation into a clear pen line. A hurried pencil squiggle, of which the exact meaning is doubtful, is of no use: trying to work out what it means only interrupts the flow of pen work.

A pen is a precise instrument and every line made with it should be drawn as evenly as possible, so that the whole length of the line is made with one complete, uninterrupted pen stroke. If the nib is lifted away from the paper, or stops moving in the middle of a stroke, a ragged or jointed line may result (Figure 16). Such a line suggests haste or carelessness on the part of the draftsman; it could be ambiguous, and it may reproduce badly. Every effort should be made to produce smooth, even, perfect lines, especially in the case of main structural lines. To avoid smudging, ink should be applied from the top left of the drawing, working across and downwards to bottom right. A clean piece of paper should be placed between the hand and the drawing surface so that it will act as a guard against any grease.

RAGGED LINES

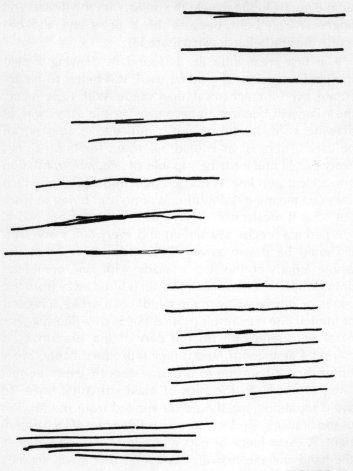

FIGURE 16

If at any stage a line cannot be made to come out right, despite repeated attempts, it may be found helpful to put the drawing away and to return to it later, or to get up and look at it from a distance. Pen and ink work is detailed work: often one cannot see the whole because of involvement in the detail. It may even be helpful to turn the drawing upside down: inversion seems to make weak or ineffective lines more noticeable. When trying to draw a particularly difficult object or trying to select the most suitable style, it may be helpful to make several different detailed pencil studies and to forget about them for a while, comparing them with the object again later on. The most suitable drawing will then stand out from the others.

● Measurement

An example is given in Figures 17 and 18 of the stages of constructing a drawing of an iron nail (somewhat idealized for the sake of simplicity) at 2/1 for reproduction at 1/1. The explanation which follows may seem tediously detailed for so simple an object as a nail but is to explain fully the methods used, which may not be instantly apparent from the illustrations. Stages 1—9 are all pencil work; ink is used for the first time at Stage 10. Let us assume that the nail is not bent, has a square shank with parallel sides which taper only at the point and a flat circular head. The shank bears a lump of corrosion about halfway down its length but is otherwise uncorroded.

The first thing to do (Stage 1) is to draw a rough sketch showing the main features to measure and to measure the length AB in millimeters. This is 35 mm. For drawing at 2/1, a vertical line of 70 mm. is drawn to represent the

STAGES OF CONSTRUCTING A DRAWING AT 2/1

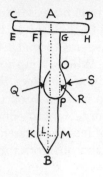

1

ROUGH SKETCH AT 1/1 WITH MEASURING POINTS NOTED

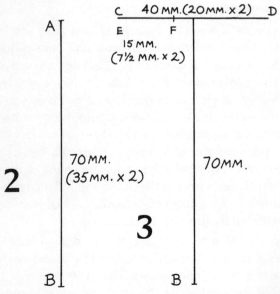

2

3

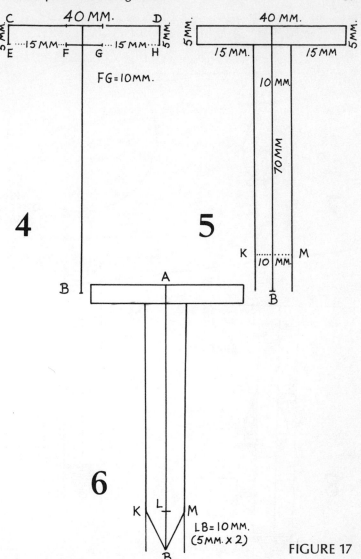

FIGURE 17

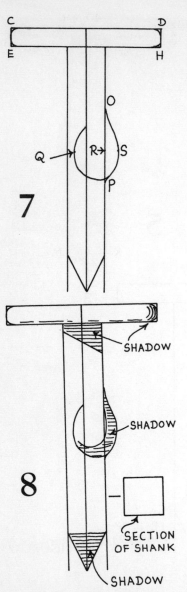

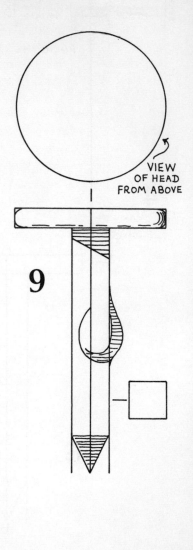

VIEW
OF HEAD
FROM ABOVE

SECTION
OF SHANK

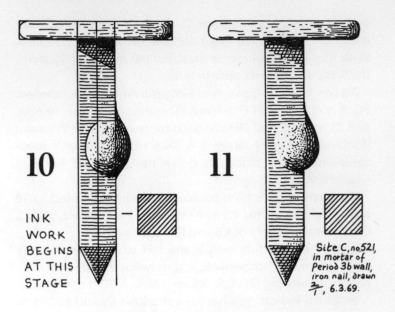

10

INK
WORK
BEGINS
AT THIS
STAGE

11

Site C, no.521,
in mortar of
Period 3b wall,
iron nail, drawn
$\frac{2}{1}$, 6.3.69.

THE
COMPLETED
DRAWING
REDUCED TO
1/1, AS WHEN
PRINTED

FIGURE 18

vertical axis. This gives Stage 2. Next we measure CD, the width of the head (20 mm.) and the distance EF, 7½ mm. With these measurements doubled (40 mm. and 15 mm.) the Stage 3 outline is constructed.

To reach Stage 4, two more measurements are needed, FG (5 mm.) and GH (7½ mm.). These doubled are 10 mm. and 15 mm. CE and DH are then measured (both 2½ mm., doubled to 5 mm.). Stage 5 is then reached, check measurements being made all down the shank of the nail (e.g. at KM).

To reach Stage 6, LB is measured (5 mm., doubled to 10 mm.) and the points K, B, M can then be joined, with a check measurement of KB and BM if desired.

Stage 7 is rounding off CE and DH to indicate that the head is circular, not square, and drawing the lump of corrosion, measuring OP, QR, RS and QRS.

Stage 8 is indicating where the shadows should go below the head and on the corroded lump and drawing the section across the square shank. at any suitable point on its length to indicate that the shank is in fact square and not a flat strip or oblong in section.

Stage 9—which is optional and perhaps unnecessary with so simple an object as a nail—is to make it quite clear that the head is round. This is, of course, obvious to the draftsman examining the nail but the roundness is not necessarily apparent to the reader of the publication in which the drawing appears—he might, unless its roundness is shown, assume that the head is square. It is not easy to decide how much extra explanatory detail of this kind is necessary in a drawing of a find: in general, it should not be necessary unless the object has features markedly different from other objects of the same kind or is distinctly unusual or rare.

After all measurements have been checked, ink work begins, with Stage 10 involving inking over all pencil lines and indicating texture (especially in the corroded area), keeping the texture lines "open."

Stage 11 is the erasing of all pencil lines, making any necessary corrections with process white or Snopake, and checking the drawing through the reducing glass. At this stage it is essential to number the completed drawing according to the find label attached to the object, or the find bag, being sure to note the scale of the drawing as well, e.g. "Site C no. 521 in mortar of Period 3b wall, iron nail, 2/1," and the date of drawing. This can be penciled on the back of the drawing or below it, and will prevent any confusion should the label or the object be mislaid. It is important to note the scale at which the drawing has been made to prevent the find from being inadvertently published at the wrong size. Numbering each drawing is particularly important if many drawings are being made together of similar objects from the same site or different sites.

This may seem a cumbrous, mechanical way of preparing a drawing of a very simple object but it demonstrates one of the most important factors in constructing an archaeological drawing—accurate measurement. Deciding exactly what to measure can be difficult and in Figure 19 the most important measuring points are indicated for a variety of objects.

DECIDING WHAT TO MEASURE

Arrows indicate the essential points

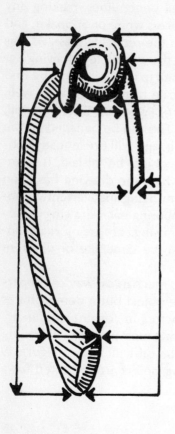

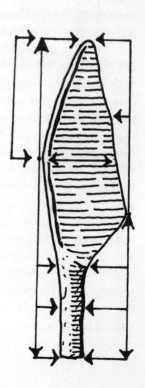

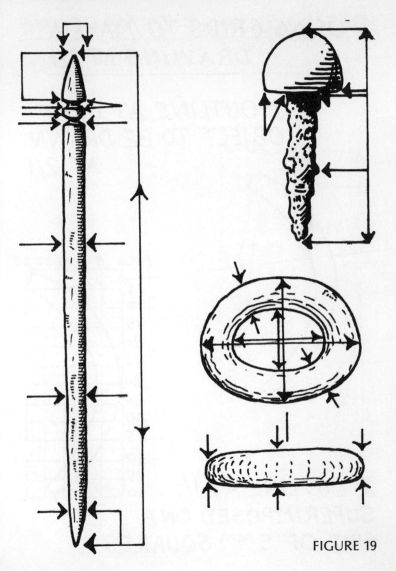

FIGURE 19

USING GRIDS TO MAKE A DRAWING AT 2/1

1 OUTLINE, AT 1/1, OF OBJECT TO BE DRAWN AT 2/1

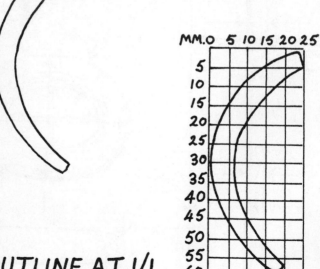

2 OUTLINE AT 1/1 SUPERIMPOSED ON A GRID OF 5ᴹᴹ SQUARES

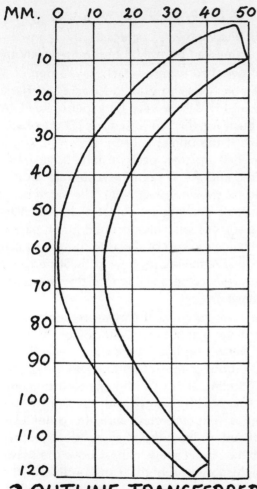

MM. 0   10   20   30   40   50

10
20
30
40
50
60
70
80
90
100
110
120

**3 OUTLINE TRANSFERRED
TO DOUBLE-SIZED GRID
OF 10ᴹᴹ SQUARES=2/1**

FIGURE 20

• Outlining

With particularly tricky objects, especially those involving curves, the outline can be established quite easily by
making a grid of penciled squares (each, say, 5 mm. X 5
mm.), laying the object on the grid and tracing its basic
outline carefully at 1/1 with a very long pencil lead. A
clutch pencil is ideal for this; so, of course, is an object
which is fairly flat. If the object is to be drawn at 2/1, a
second grid of pencil squares, each 10 mm. X 10 mm.,
should be prepared and the 1/1 outline scaled up on this
double-sized grid, as shown in Figure 20. The same prin-
ciple can be used for drawing an object at less than its
actual size. If two sorts of faint blue printed graph paper,
one with squares twice the size of those of the other, can
be obtained, it will save having to draw grids of penciled
squares. The engraver's camera will ignore the faint blue
lines on the graph paper.

Care should be taken to check the measurement of the
1/1 outline against the actual object and to see that the
measurements of the 2/1 outline on the double-sized grid
are exactly double those of the 1/1 outline and the object
itself. A penciled outline at 2/1 can be checked by comparing the object seen with one eye with the drawn outline seen through a reducing glass with the other eye.
This is more difficult to describe than to do. Another
method is to hold the object a few inches above the drawing, looking straight down on both. If the outline of the
object and the outline of the drawing coincide exactly, it
can be assumed that the drawn outline is accurate. If the
drawn outline is at variance with the outline of the object,
then obviously the drawn outline needs to be altered. A

third method is to hold the object a few inches above the drawing and to position a lamp above both so that the clearly defined shadow of the object is cast on the drawing. The cast shadow should tally exactly with the outline of the drawing if the drawing has been accurately made.

● Shading and Hatching

The need to keep shading and hatching "open" has been mentioned on page 19 and needs further consideration. There is a very limited range of shading at our disposal between pure white and absolute black and we need to be able to exploit this limited range to the greatest effect. The beginner, however, would be well advised to limit his shading to the four kinds shown in Figure 21. Of these the cross-hatching shown in no. 4 should be used sparingly— it can easily turn into solid black if the drawing is greatly reduced in size in making the engravings. For most purposes the shading and cross-hatching shown in nos. 1, 2 and 3 are adequate.

Shading should be applied so that it cannot be confused with the basic structural lines of the drawing and so that it does not clash with the shape which is being represented. This is explained in more detail in Figure 22. If, for any reason, it is imperative that shading lines should run parallel to structural lines, the structural lines should be drawn with a thicker nib than is employed for the shading. Indeed, for clarity in any drawing it is worth considering the use of a thick nib for structural lines and a thinner nib for shading.

Closely bound up with the problem of shading and hatching to show modeling is the problem of showing the sur-

BASIC SHADING AND
CROSS-HATCHING (shown unreduced)

1.- Simple shading drawn in one direction only. Dark tones can be suggested by placing the lines closer, as in __A__, without resorting to cross-hatching.

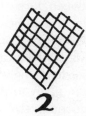

2.- Cross-hatching, two sets of strokes at opposing angles will, with __1__, suffice for many simple drawings, as in __B__.

3.- Cross-hatching with three sets of strokes at different angles. will, in many cases, serve for the very darkest shadows (__C__).

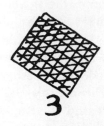

4.- Cross-hatching with four sets of strokes is not often needed and tends to "fill in" badly in reduction.

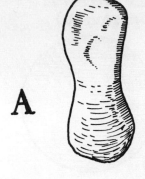

A

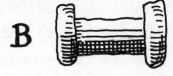

B

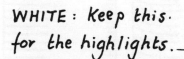

C

WHITE: Keep this.
for the highlights.

BLACK: Use sparingly
for the darkest accents.

FIGURE 21

SHADING AND SHAPE
(all shown unreduced)

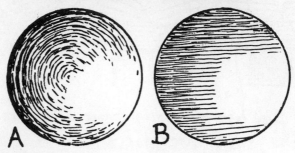

A   B

SUGGESTION OF SHAPE

In A and C the curved lines of
the shading help to reinforce the impression
of roundness, but in B and D the straight
shading lines deny it. Where possible, try
to apply lines so that they actively aid
representation
of shape.

C   D

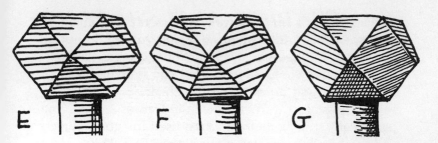

In E the use of similar horizontal shading to show all the facets does not aid the representation of shape. F is more successful in this and G looks better than F —— except that the areas of close shading in G may reproduce badly when the drawing is reduced.

In H structural and shading lines are too alike for the shape to be clear. In I the shape is clearer.

FIGURE 22

face texture of a find. Showing surface texture enhances
the appearance and value of a drawing but should not be
overdone. Care must be taken that lines representing texture cannot be confused with the basic structural lines of
the drawing and do not clog the shadows. Examples of
various possible textures are given in Figures 23—25. One
particularly striking method, often used for stone objects
and sometimes for metal, is stipple and dot. This is most
effective for showing texture and shading together, if
done carefully, but is most time-consuming. If stipple and
dot is used for shading, particular care has to be taken,
when showing the roundness of a round object, to make a
light area containing only a few dots merge gently and almost imperceptibly with a dark area containing many dots
to avoid giving the appearance of a sudden angular transition (Figure 26A). In large areas of even stippling regular
patterns should not be allowed to develop because these
stand out oddly (Figure 26C). Dot sizes should also be
carefully chosen to suit the proposed degree of reduction
(Figure 27). With bone objects a realistic effect is given if
the shading runs vertically in thin lines and stipple and dot
is used for abraded surfaces (Figure 25). Glass objects pre-
sent much difficulty over showing surface texture. Stipple
and dot is suitable for some glass surfaces. Any naturally
black object—e.g. jet—gives difficulty over showing shadows, surface texture and color. It is sometimes possible to
give a good representation of color by painting the whole
drawing over with India ink and picking out the structural lines thinly with process white or Snopake, but not
all objects are suited to this treatment (see jet bead,
Figure 23). The general rule for all classes of finds should

be to play for safety: surface texture is best omitted if it interferes with clarity. It is, however, worth trying a few experiments before plumping for the easiest way out. Much can be learned by making three or four attempts at showing the same object in different ways.

• Indicating Colors

When drawing objects—e.g. brooches—decorated with colored enameling, it may be found helpful to employ conventions used in heraldry to indicate colors: vertical shading for red, horizontal shading for blue, oblique shading from top right to bottom left for green, oblique shading from top left to bottom right for purple, stippling for yellow, vertical and horizontal cross-hatching for black, and no shading at all for white or silver (Figure 28). A similar method—or the method shown in Figure 25—can be used for colored wall plaster. An explanatory key should be added to the drawing.

Apart from showing modeling and, if possible, surface texture, a drawing should also indicate the construction of an object by showing sections through it. All that is required is measurement at appropriate points. For example, if the shank of a pin is square in section for part of its length and round for the other part, square and round sections should be drawn beside the relevant parts. Some objects may need to be shown in two different aspects, from the front and from the side. It is customary to show brooches, for example, from the front and from the side; frontal drawings alone are inadequate to demonstrate their structure. Some finds may need to be shown from three aspects (front, back and side)—or even from

TEXTURE AND TREATMENT—1
(all shown unreduced)

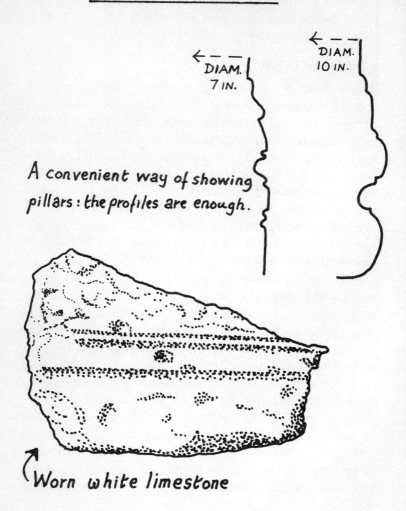

← -- DIAM. 7 IN.

← -- DIAM. 10 IN.

A convenient way of showing pillars : the profiles are enough.

↰ Worn white limestone

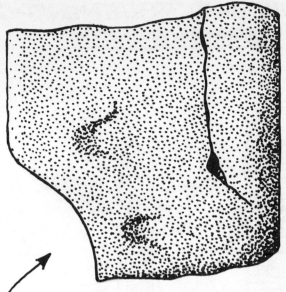

Close-grained polished dark stone

Worked jet

—Jet bead—
A shows the
color but
not the shape:
B is more
informative.

A   B

FIGURE 23

TEXTURE AND TREATMENT—2
(all shown unreduced)

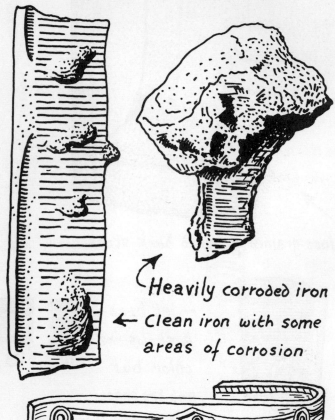

↳ Heavily corroded iron

← Clean iron with some
areas of corrosion

↖ Patterned bronze — surface
texture has to be omitted to show pattern.

A & B →
A convenient
way of showing
a pattern on a
ring or bracelet.
B = as found; A=
pattern "rolled
out flat."

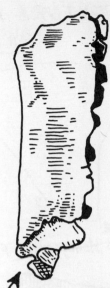

Lead sheet

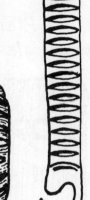

B   A

← Plain bronze

FIGURE 24

TEXTURE AND TREATMENT—3
(all shown unreduced)

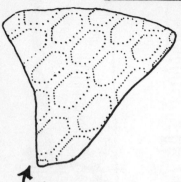

↑ Honeycomb patterned glass

Plain glass beads

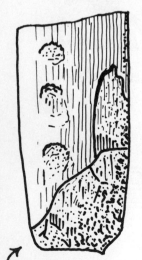

↑ Roughly trimmed bone

↑ Polished bone

↑ Trimmed bone
(wood can be
shown similarly)

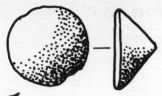

↖ Cone of dark glass

Painted wall
plaster.

↖ Roughly cut
bone ring

WHITE ☐ GREEN
RED BLACK ▮

A color key should
be given, as here.

FIGURE 25

STIPPLE AND DOT

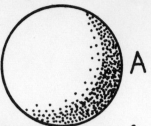

A

Here the transition from
light to dark is too abrupt.

Here the transition is
more gentle and natural.

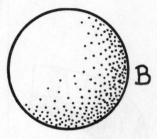

B

Here regular — and
distracting — patterns
have been allowed to
develop.

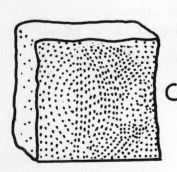

C

FIGURE 26

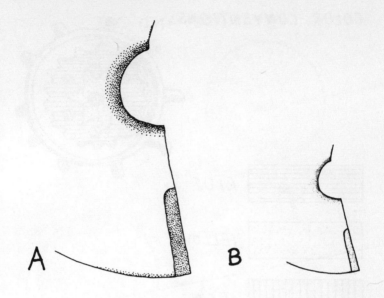

Dot size should be
chosen to suit the
proposed degree of
reduction. The dots
in A are too small to
withstand reduction
to ½ as in B.

FIGURE 27

COLOR CONVENTIONS

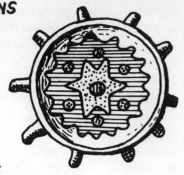

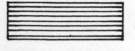 BLUE

YELLOW

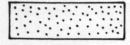 RED

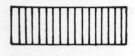 GREEN

PURPLE

 BLACK

 WHITE
OR SILVER

FIGURE 28

more than three, perhaps from above, below, front, back, and both sides. If the space available for the drawing does not allow such detailed treatment a perspective drawing may be necessary.

Making a perspective drawing can be difficult and time-consuming. One solution is to have the object photographed and to use the photograph as a basis for a drawing. The outline of the object can be inked over on the photograph and then traced onto tracing paper. This method (a variation of which is described on p. 89), although rather roundabout, has the virtue of accuracy. A more direct method, which may however prove a good deal more difficult and irritating at first for the beginner, is to set the object up and then, literally, draw what is seen, using a ruler to note the distances between various points on the object and transferring these measurements to a penciled grid of squares on the drawing paper. Angles can be judged by eye or by tilting the ruler and noting the angle.

FINISHING TOUCHES

When drawing a large number of objects to be shown together in one text figure, it is not necessary—and often it is quite impossible—to try to draw them all on the same piece of paper. Indeed, it is not desirable to attempt to do so because, until the set of drawings has been completed, it is almost impossible to judge exactly how much space can be allotted to each individual drawing. If each drawing is made on a separate piece of paper and the surplus is trimmed away, leaving about one-quarter inch of blank paper round each, the individual drawings can be juggled about on a larger sheet to determine the best positions for them all and then pasted in place. As we have seen, the engraver's camera will pick out only the black lines and will ignore the white patchwork. Difficulty in deciding on the best positioning of each drawing can be overcome by making a dummy on thin layout paper (which is cheaper than tracing paper) and tracing the outlines of all the drawings roughly in an area of the same size as will be available for them in the finished drawing (e.g. an area 14 in. X 10 in. if the drawings were all made at 2/1 for reduction to 1/1 to fill a text figure which is to be 7

in. X 5 in. when published). Several tentative arrange-
ments can be worked out in this way and, when a choice
has been finally made, the drawings can be pasted on
mounting board, using the dummy as a guide. The border,
if the figure is to have a border, can then be inked in on
the mounting board.

Borders are best drawn as plain lines—nothing elaborate or ornate is required or desirable. The frame is not
more important than the picture. Borders are not always
necessary but can set off a drawing well. They will help
to hold together a large group of small separate drawings.
Border lines should be drawn fairly thick because they
are isolated, unsupported lines; if they are drawn very
thin they may reproduce badly in the engraving.

● Grouping Drawings

Separate drawings can be pasted surprisingly close together in a big text figure without making the page
seem overcrowded when it has been reduced. Although
they may seem alarmingly close in the original, the effect
of reduction is to appear to increase the amount of white
space between each. Because line engravings are expensive every effort should be made to fill a text figure
without waste. This means placing drawings close to the
borders. The amount of space left at the bottom of a text
figure should be a little greater than the space left at the
top, particularly if there are many drawings in the figure.
If this is not done, the illusion can be given that the objects are "falling out of the picture."

If any of the individual drawings in a composite text
figure have been made on Bristol board or thick paper,

it is advisable to paint round and over their edges with process white or Snopake after they have been pasted in place. The thickness of Bristol board or paper can cast a shadow which may be seen by the engraver's camera as a black line.

To complete a figure comprising several individual drawings, it is necessary to number the drawings and to add a scale. It may also be necessary to add explanatory lettering. Unless one can draw really good, consistent numerals and letters with the pen—which demands much practice and skill, particularly with very large sizes of lettering, and a plain rather than an elaborate style—it is best to use a stencil or dry transfer lettering such as Letraset or Formatt. Most stencils, however, yield utilitarian if not downright ugly lettering and numerals, and much more elegant lettering of all kinds is available in Letraset and Formatt. Care should be taken to select a style of lettering which suits the drawing and, after consulting the editor of the publication in which the drawing will appear, the kind of type face likely to be used for the text. For example, the more exotic and grotesque styles, such as Old English or Egyptian, should be avoided; they draw too much attention to themselves. There are plenty of good, sober styles from which to choose (Figure 29).

● Lettering

Whatever lettering is used must, of course, be sufficiently large to withstand the intended degree of reduction of the drawing on which it appears. Groups of words and the individual letters in words should be placed close to-

FINISHING TOUCHES

66   67   68

Hand-drawn numerals,
reduced here to ½

Dry transfer numerals

58

A

B   58

A (16 pt. or 4.5mm size)
will reduce to ½, as in
B, but would be hard
to read if reduced to ¼.

45 This size
(36pt. or 9.5mm)
will reduce to ¼ but
would be too large at ½.

Two unsuitable styles

123 48

FIGURE 29

gether for the neatest results. Correct spacing of capital letters is a matter of adjusting the spacing so as to give a visual appearance of equal space throughout a word. For example, the letters A, T, V, W, Y require less space on either side of them than upright letters such as H, I, M, N, and the letters L and P need less space after them than before them. The space required for any lettering should, of course, be worked out carefully in pencil, with a ruler, before the lettering is applied. If a fair amount of explanatory lettering needs to be added to a drawing, it is best applied to a separate piece of paper which can be trimmed and pasted on to the drawing. This saves having to mess the drawing about if one is dissatisfied with the completed lettering.

It is not always necessary to add a drawn scale to a drawing, particularly if the caption indicates clearly the size of the objects shown in the drawing. Errors can, however, occur in captions and there is no harm in including a scale in a drawing. If the drawings are all made at 2/1, the scale must also be drawn at 2/1. It is customary to show the scale in both inches and millimeters or centimeters. A scale should be unobtrusive and of simple line construction (Figure 30). If several objects are shown in one text figure at different scales, several different scales will need to be included, each closely related to the object to which it refers.

Before a drawing leaves the draftsman's hands, everything in it should be checked carefully. The link lines joining the frontal and side views of each object should not be forgotten and all numbering of objects in the drawing should be checked. It is very easy to omit a number

SIMPLE SCALES
(reduced here to ¼)

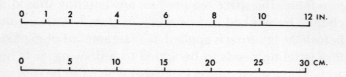

FIGURE 30

The line engraving for
this was made from
a completely unaltered
photocopy of the
original drawing.

FIGURE 31

by mistake. A photocopy should be made of the drawing;
if the original is lost it may be less troublesome to turn
a photocopy into a replacement than to draw the object
all over again (Figure 31).

DRAWINGS FROM PHOTOGRAPHS

In most excavations a good many photographs are taken which are not reproduced in the final report because of the cost of halftone engravings. Although there are several purely photographic processes by which black-and-white photographic negatives can be induced to yield prints approximating to line drawings, they tend to be expensive and tedious and the results are not always suitable for line reproduction. Line drawings can, however, be produced quite simply from negatives, or from color slides, if a photographic enlarger or a slide projector is available.

The method is this: darken the room, fasten drawing paper to the enlarger baseboard, put the negative in the enlarger and focus it at whatever image size is required and then trace the outlines of the projected image on the drawing paper. The tracing can then be worked up into as simple or elaborate a line drawing as may be desired.

One disadvantage of using a black-and-white negative in this way is that the tone values are, of course, reversed, which can lead to confusion between highlights and shadows in negatives of complex objects, but this can be over-

DRAWINGS FROM PHOTOGRAPHIC NEGATIVES

BROKEN PILLAR

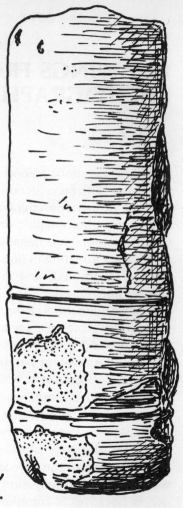

Early stage of drawing, shown here unreduced.

HEARTHS

(shown here reduced to ½)

FIGURE 32

come by common sense and by checking against a print from the negative. A disadvantage of using an enlarger as a projector is that the negative may buckle if exposed for many minutes to the heat of the enlarger lamphouse. If a suitable means of suspension (e.g. a stepladder on a table) can be devised to allow easy alteration of the size of the projected image, a slide projector can be used instead of an enlarger. The drawings of hearths in Figure 32 were made from photographic negatives projected for about three minutes in an enlarger—long enough to decide on the size of drawing required to fill the space available for each and to trace the basic outlines in pencil—and the drawing of the pillar was made from a black-and-white 35 mm. transparency.

One great advantage of using a negative (or a color slide or black-and-white lantern slide) in this way is that irrelevant features recorded on the negative by the camera can be omitted from the drawing and particularly important features can, if necessary, be emphasized.

For the best results, particularly if a large drawing is to be made, the most suitable negative is one which is rather underexposed and "thin." A dense, overexposed negative does not yield so clear an image. The general rule seems to be: "if it would make a good enlargement on normal grade photographic paper, it should be easy to make a drawing from it."

A line drawing can also be made from a photographic print by drawing over the print in India ink and then bleaching out the photographic image: with this method, however, the size of the drawing is entirely dependent on the size of the photographic print. Using a negative or slide in an enlarger or projector means that there is no such restriction on the size of the final drawing: the negative or slide can be projected at whatever size may be desired.

SUMMING UP

Drawings will be effective if the following points are constantly borne in mind:

1. Accuracy, especially over detail, is essential; this entails close observation and precise measurement.

2. Clean, clear lines, drawn in an open style, reproduce best.

3. The finishing touches—e.g. lettering and removal of blemishes—are most important and can make or mar a drawing.

4. Regular practice in drawing objects—any objects—is the best teacher and will rapidly improve your technique. "Never a day without a line" is sound counsel.

5. Much can be learned from studying other people's drawings. The line illustrations in, for example, the Research Reports of the Society of Antiquaries and publications of equally high standard are most informative and very well worth studying.

6. Do not be easily satisfied with what you have done, unless you are quite sure you can do no better. Aim at perfection and think always of your reader. Does your drawing tell him all he needs to know? To him the

printed result is all that matters. He is interested only in the object you are illustrating for him, not in how long it took you or what pains it cost you.

If you become discouraged, remember that as a still-life draftsman you have an immense advantage over the portrait or landscape artist. Your subject cannot change its expression, move, or be subtly altered by weather, the vagaries of the seasons or the varying intensity of light. You do not have to hurry; you can always try again if you are not satisfied.